the
poetry
of
Emily
Dickinson

ISBN
9781788287715

W0008625

the poetry of Emily Dickinson

This edition published in 2019 by Arcturus Publishing Limited
26/27 Bickels Yard, 151–153 Bermondsey Street,
London SE1 3HA

Copyright © Arcturus Holdings Limited

All rights reserved. No part of this publication may be reproduced,
stored in a retrieval system, or transmitted, in any form or by any
means, electronic, mechanical, photocopying, recording or otherwise,
without prior written permission in accordance with the provisions of
the Copyright Act 1956 (as amended). Any person or persons who do
any unauthorised act in relation to this publication may be liable to
criminal prosecution and civil claims for damages.

AD006340US

Printed in the UK

Contents

Introduction

Barely published in her own lifetime, in death Emily Dickinson achieved a posthumous fame unparalleled in American literary history. But for her sister, Lavinia, it is doubtful that her poems would ever have been printed. However, when the first volume was published four years after her death, it met with stunning success, going through eleven editions in less than two years.

Emily was born in Amherst, Massachusetts, in December 1830. The Dickinsons' house, the Homestead on Main Street, was the center of Amherst society. The young Emily was a brilliant student with great social flair. She was full of gaiety and wit and regularly "rode out" with suitors, though nothing came of these attachments.

In an era of religious revivals, Emily's interests were firmly set towards science and nature. In 1847, she attended Mount Holyoke Female Seminary, an establishment with a strong tradition of evangelical Christianity. Years later a fellow student, Clara Turner, recalled the moment when the headmistress "asked all those who wanted to be Christians to rise." Emily remained seated. No one else did. Turner reports Emily's comment to her: "'They thought it queer I didn't rise' – adding with a twinkle in her eye, 'I thought a lie would be queerer.'"

With her formal education at an end, Emily was required to take up the social niceties of her station: domestic duties and daily rounds of social visits. But Emily refused to participate, instead baking bread, gardening, or writing letters. She was a vigorous letter writer, some scholars speculating that this was a kind of "visiting without distraction."

In 1856, her brother Austin married a close friend of Emily's, Susan Gilbert, and the couple built a house next door called the Evergreens. This small family enclave was perfect for the retiring Emily and inspired the start of a creative streak. By the age of 36, she had written more than a thousand poems, many of them copied out in small self-made booklets and stored in her writing desk. Her poems were widely read by her friends and correspondents—Susan Gilbert received over 200 poems in letters from Emily—but hardly ever published. This was a normal part of women's literary culture in the 19th century.

Scholars have long been intrigued by the sudden creative outpouring, giving rise to a "before and after" theory set around an invisible catastrophe or "terror" that Emily referred to in some of her letters. Some suggest a failed romantic liaison or a nervous illness, but recently there has been compelling evidence that she suffered from epilepsy, a condition which existed in the family and one that elicited shame during those years, usually dealt with in private by lifelong silence.

Whatever prompted it, at this point Emily's poems had a new-found confidence. Her unique, style was simple, to the point, and expressive. Many take on the cadence and rhythm of hymns with four-beat and three-beat lines. Using light almost jaunty language, they address lofty themes with great power: the soul, love, rebellion, freedom, salvation, escape, and death, her sweet tone often masking deep meaning and intense emotion. That these subjects should be so shrewdly observed by a reclusive, birdlike spinster, speaks volumes about the character of someone who had the courage to reject God.

In 1862, she sent examples of her work to Thomas Higginson in response to an article in *Atlantic Monthly*. A well-known literary figure, Higginson was not exactly effusive in his praise of her work and, in turn, she took little notice of his advice, but they began a correspondence that would last for the rest of Emily's life.

In the mid-1860s, Emily suffered eye problems, staying with relations in Boston while undergoing treatment. She returned home in late 1865 and rarely ventured again beyond the grounds of the Homestead until her death 20 years later.

A traumatic event occurred in 1881 when her brother, Austin, had an affair with Mabel Loomis Todd, a 27-year-old beauty newly arrived from Washington. Rejecting his wife, Susan, Emily's friend and confidante for so long, he split the family in two. Austin took against his children, who sided with their mother; Lavinia sided with the lovers. The feud continued and still raged when Emily died, of Bright's disease, in 1886.

Shortly after Emily's death, Lavinia found a cache of some 1,700 poems and hundreds of letters. She gave the material to Mabel Todd, who became increasingly enthusiastic about the beauty and power of the poems she read. With the help and encouragement of Thomas Higginson, the first edition of poems was published in 1890. They received extraordinary praise from leading magazines and newspapers. The *New York Times* claimed Emily Dickinson would soon be among the immortals of English-speaking poets. That they were not wrong is borne out by this intriguing and beautiful collection, which includes some of her finest and most significant works. Even today the bold voice of her poems can't be categorized: "I'm Nobody," says Emily, "—who are you?" Hers is a voice that can't be ignored, confrontational, even invasive, with a piercing question about our being.

There is another sky
Ever serene and fair,
And there is another sunshine,
Though it be darkness there —
Never mind faded forests, Austin,
Never mind silent fields —
Here is a little forest
Whose leaf is ever green —
Here is a brighter garden —
Where not a frost has been,
In its unfading flowers
I hear the bright bee hum,
Prithee, my Brother,
Into my garden come!

∽

Awake ye muses nine, sing me a strain divine,
Unwind the solemn twine, and tie my Valentine!

Oh the Earth was made for lovers, for damsel, and
    hopeless swain,
For sighing, and gentle whispering, and unity made of
    twain.
All things do go a courting, in earth, or sea, or air,
God hath made nothing single but thee in His world so
    fair!

The bride, and then the bridegroom, the two, and then
  the one,
Adam, and Eve, his consort, the moon, and then the sun;
The life doth prove the precept, who obey shall happy be,
Who will not serve the sovereign, be hanged on fatal
  tree.
The high do seek the lowly, the great do seek the small,
None cannot find who seeketh, on this terrestrial ball;
The bee doth court the flower, the flower his suit receives,
And they make merry wedding, whose guests are
  hundred leaves;
The wind doth woo the branches, the branches they
  are won,
And the father fond demandeth the maiden for his son.
The storm doth walk the seashore humming a
  mournful tune,
The wave with eye so pensive, looketh to see the
  moon,
Their spirits meet together, they make their solemn
  vows,
No more he singeth mournful, her sadness she doth
  lose.
The worm doth woo the mortal, death claims a living
  bride,
Night unto day is married, morn unto eventide;
Earth is a merry damsel, and heaven a knight so true,
And Earth is quite coquettish, and beseemeth in vain to
  sue.
Now to the application, to the reading of the roll,
To bringing thee to justice, and marshalling thy soul:
Thou art a human solo, a being cold, and lone,

Wilt have no kind companion, thou reap'st what thou
  hast sown.
Hast never silent hours, and minutes all too long,
And a deal of sad reflection, and wailing instead of
  song?
There's Sarah, and Eliza, and Emeline so fair,
And Harriet, and Susan, and she with curling hair!
Thine eyes are sadly blinded, but yet thou mayest see
Six true, and comely maidens sitting upon the tree;
Approach that tree with caution, then up it boldly
  climb,
And seize the one thou lovest, nor care for space, or
  time!
Then bear her to the greenwood, and build for her a
  bower,
And give her what she asketh, jewel, or bird, or flower
  —

And bring the fife, and trumpet, and beat upon the
  drum —
And bid the world Goodmorrow, and go to glory
  home!

꼬

"Sic transit gloria mundi"
"How doth the busy bee"
"Dum vivamus vivamus"
I stay mine enemy! —

Oh "veni vidi vici!"
Oh caput cap-a-pie!
And oh "memento mori"
When I am far from thee!

Hurrah for Peter Parley!
Hurrrah for Daniel Boone!
Three cheers, sir, for the gentleman
Who first observed the moon —

Peter put up the sunshine!
Pattie arrange the stars
Tell Luna, tea is waiting
And call your brother Mars!

Put down the apple, Adam,
And come away with me,
So shalt thou have a pippin
From off my Father's tree!

I climb the "Hill of Science"
I "view the Landscape o'er;"
Such transcendental prospect
I ne'er beheld before!

Unto the Legislature
My country bids me go;
I'll take my india rubbers,
In case the wind should blow!

During my education,
It was announced to me
That gravitation stumbling,
Fell from an apple tree!

The Earth upon an axis
Was once supposed to turn,
By way of a gymnastic
In honor to the sun!

It was the brave Columbus,
A sailing o'er the tide,
Who notified the nations
Of where I would reside!

Mortality is fatal,
Gentility is fine,
Rascality, heroic,
Insolvency, sublime!

Our Fathers being weary,
Laid down on Bunker Hill,
And tho' full many a morning
Yet they are sleeping still!

The trumpet, sir, shall wake them,
In streams I see them rise,
Each with a solemn musket
A marching to the skies!

A coward will remain, Sir,
Until the fight is done;
But an immortal hero
Will take his hat, and run.

Good bye, Sir, I am going;
My country calleth me;
Allow me, Sir, at parting,
To wipe my weeping e'e.

In token of our friendship
Accept this "Bonnie Doon,"
And when the hand that pluck'd it
Hath passed beyond the moon,

The memory of my ashes
Will consolation be;
Then farewell Tuscarora,
And farewell, Sir, to thee!

∽

On this wondrous sea
Sailing silently,
Ho! Pilot, ho!
Knowest thou the shore
Where no breakers roar,
Where the storm is o'er?

In the peaceful west
Many the sails at rest —
The anchors fast —
Thither I pilot thee!
Land Ho! Eternity!
Ashore at last!

ᥫᤁ

I have a Bird in spring
Which for myself doth sing —
The spring decoys.
And as the summer nears —
And as the Rose appears,
Robin is gone.

Yet do I not repine
Knowing that Bird of mine
Though flown —
Learneth beyond the sea
Melody new for me
And will return.

Fast in safer hand
Held in a truer Land
Are mine —
And though they now depart,

Tell I my doubting heart
They're thine.

In a serener Bright,
In a more golden light
I see
Each little doubt and fear,
Each little discord here
Removed.

Then will I not repine,
Knowing that Bird of mine
Though flown
Shall in distant tree
Bright melody for me
Return.

⌒

Oh if remembering were forgetting —
Then I remember not!
And if forgetting — recollecting —
How near I had forgot!
And if to miss — were merry —
And to mourn were gay,
How very blithe the maiden
Who gathered these today!

~∽

Nobody knows this little rose;
It might a pilgrim be,
Did I not take it from the ways,
And lift it up to thee!

Only a bee will miss it;
Only a butterfly,
Hastening from far journey,
On it's breast to lie.

Only a bird will wonder;
Only a breeze will sigh;
Ah! little rose, how easy
For such as thee to die!

~∽

The feet of people walking home
With gayer sandals go —
The crocus — till she rises —
The vassal of the snow —
The lips at Hallelujah
Long years of practise bore —
Till bye and bye, these Bargemen
Walked — singing — on the shore

Pearls are the Diver's farthings
Extorted form the sea —
Pinions — the Seraph's wagon —
Pedestrian once — as we —
Night is the morning's canvas —
Larceny — legacy —
Death — but our rapt attention
To immortality.

My figures fail to tell me
How far the village lies —
Whose peasants are the angels —
Whose cantons dot the skies —
My Classics vail their faces —
My faith that Dark adores —
Which from its solemn abbeys —
Such resurrection pours!

∽

If those I loved were lost,
the crier's voice would tell me —
If those I loved were found,
the bells of Ghent would ring,

Did those I loved repose,
the Daisy would impel me —

Philip when bewildered —
bore his riddle in —

◌

Frequently the woods are pink —
Frequently are brown.
Frequently the hills undress
Behind my native town.
Oft a head is crested
I was wont to see —
And as oft a cranny
Where it used to be —
And the Earth — they tell me —
On its axis turned!
Wonderful Rotation!
By but twelve performed!

◌

We lose — because we win —
Gamblers — recollecting which
Toss their dice again!

Taken from men — this morning —
Carried by men today —
Met by the Gods with banners —
Who marshalled her away —

One little maid — from playmates —
One little mind from school —
There must be guests in Eden —
All the rooms are full —

Far — as the East from Even —
Dim — as the border star —
Courtiers quaint, in Kingdoms
Our departed are.

If I should die,
And you should live —
And time should gurgle on —
And morn should beam —
And noon should burn —
As it has usual done —
If Birds should build as early

And Bees as bustling go —
One might depart at option
From enterprise below!
'Tis sweet to know that stocks will stand
When we with Daisies lie —
That Commerce will continue —
And Trades as briskly fly —
It makes the parting tranquil
And keeps the soul serene —
That gentlemen so sprightly
Conduct the pleasing scene!

&

I haven't told my garden yet —
Lest that should conquer me.
I haven't quite the strength now
To break it to the Bee —

I will not name it in the street
For shops would stare at me —
That one so shy — so ignorant
Should have the face to die.

The hillsides must not know it —
Where I have rambled so —
Nor tell the loving forests
The day that I shall go —

Nor lisp it at the table —
Nor heedless by the way
Hint that within the Riddle
One will walk today —

ᧁ

I often passed the village
When going home from school —
And wondered what they did there —
And why it was so still —

I did not know the year then —
In which my call would come —
Earlier, by the Dial,
Than the rest have gone.

It's stiller than the sundown.
It's cooler than the dawn —
The Daisies dare to come here —
And birds can flutter down —

So when you are tired —
Or perplexed — or cold —
Trust the loving promise
Underneath the mould,
Cry "it's I," "take Dollie,"
And I will enfold!

I counted till they danced so
Their slippers leaped the town,
And then I took a pencil
To note the rebels down.
And then they grew so jolly
I did resign the prig,
And ten of my once stately toes
Are marshalled for a jig!

Whose cheek is this?
What rosy face
Has lost a blush today?
I found her — "pleiad" — in the woods
And bore her safe away.

Robins, in the tradition
Did cover such with leaves,
But which the cheek —
And which the pall
My scrutiny deceives.

It did not surprise me —
So I said — or thought —
She will stir her pinions
And the nest forgot,

Traverse broader forests —
Build in gayer boughs,
Breathe in Ear more modern
God's old fashioned vows —

This was but a Birdling —
What and if it be
One within my bosom
Had departed me?

This was but a story —
What and if indeed
There were just such coffin
In the heart instead?

Bless God, he went as soldiers,
His musket on his breast —

Grant God, he charge the bravest
Of all the martial blest!

Please God, might I behold him
In epauletted white —
I should not fear the foe then —
I should not fear the fight!

∽

To venerate the simple days
Which lead the seasons by,
Needs but to remember
That from you or I,
They may take the trifle
Termed mortality!

∽

I robbed the Woods —
The trusting Woods.
The unsuspecting Trees
Brought out their Burs and mosses
My fantasy to please.
I scanned their trinkets curious — I grasped — I bore
    away —

What will the solemn Hemlock —
What will the Oak tree say?

⁓

A Day! Help! Help! Another Day!
Your prayers, oh Passer by!
From such a common ball as this
Might date a Victory!
From marshallings as simple
The flags of nations swang.
Steady — my soul: What issues
Upon thine arrow hang!

⁓

If she had been the Mistletoe
And I had been the Rose —
How gay upon your table
My velvet life to close —
Since I am of the Druid,
And she is of the dew —
I'll deck Tradition's buttonhole —
And send the Rose to you.

~∽

There's something quieter than sleep
Within this inner room!
It wears a sprig upon its breast —
And will not tell its name.

Some touch it, and some kiss it —
Some chafe its idle hand —
It has a simple gravity
I do not understand!

I would not weep if I were they —
How rude in one to sob!
Might scare the quiet fairy
Back to her native wood!

While simple-hearted neighbors
Chat of the "Early dead" —
We — prone to periphrasis
Remark that Birds have fled!

~∽

Heart! We will forget him!
You and I — tonight!

You may forget the warmth he gave —
I will forget the light!

When you have done, pray tell me
That I may straight begin!
Haste! lest while you're lagging
I remember him!

So bashful when I spied her,
So pretty, so ashamed!
So hidden in her leaflets,
Lest anybody find;

So breathless till I passed her,
So helpless when I turned
And bore her, struggling, blushing,
Her simple haunts beyond!

For whom I robbed the dingle,
For whom betrayed the dell,
Many will doubtless ask me,
But I shall never tell!

Angels in the early morning
May be seen the dews among,
Stooping, plucking, smiling, flying:
Do the buds to them belong?

Angels when the sun is hottest
May be seen the sands among,
Stooping, plucking, sighing, flying;
Parched the flowers they bear along.

The rainbow never tells me
That gust and storm are by,
Yet is she more convincing
Than Philosophy.

My flowers turn from Forums —
Yet eloquent declare
What Cato couldn't prove me
Except the birds were here!

New feet within my garden go,
New fingers stir the sod;
A troubadour upon the elm
Betrays the solitude.

New children play upon the green,
New weary sleep below;
And still the pensive spring returns,
And still the punctual snow!

∽

For every Bird a Nest —
Wherefore in timid quest
Some little Wren goes seeking round —

Wherefore when boughs are free —
Households in every tree —
Pilgrim be found?

Perhaps a home too high —
Ah Aristocracy!
The little Wren desires —

Perhaps of twig so fine —
Of twine e'en superfine,
Her pride aspires —

The Lark is not ashamed
To build upon the ground
Her modest house —

Yet who of all the throng
Dancing around the sun
Does so rejoice?

ᥴᢁ

Soul, Wilt thou toss again?
By just such a hazard
Hundreds have lost indeed —
But tens have won an all —

Angel's breathless ballot
Lingers to record thee —
Imps in eager Caucus
Raffle for my Soul!

ᥴᢁ

Water, is taught by thirst.
Land — by the Oceans passed.
Transport — by throe —

Peace — by its battles told —
Love, by Memorial Mold —
Birds, by the Snow.

~

Good night, because we must,
How intricate the dust!
I would go, to know!
Oh incognito!
Saucy, Saucy Seraph
To elude me so!
Father! they won't tell me,
Won't you tell them to?

~

South Winds jostle them —
Bumblebees come —
Hover — hesitate —
Drink, and are gone —

Butterflies pause
On their passage Cashmere —

I — softly plucking,
Present them here!

∽

What Inn is this
Where for the night
Peculiar Traveller comes?
Who is the Landlord?
Where the maids?
Behold, what curious rooms!
No ruddy fires on the hearth —
No brimming Tankards flow —
Necromancer! Landlord!
Who are these below?

∽

My friend attacks my friend!
Oh Battle picturesque!
Then I turn Soldier too,
And he turns Satirist!
How martial is this place!
Had I a mighty gun

I think I'd shoot the human race
And then to glory run!

⌖

Success is counted sweetest
By those who ne'er succeed.
To comprehend a nectar
Requires sorest need.

Not one of all the purple host
Who took the flag to-day
Can tell the definition,
So clear, of victory,

As he, defeated, dying,
On whose forbidden ear
The distant strains of triumph
Break, agonized and clear.

⌖

"Arcturus" is his other name —
I'd rather call him "Star."
It's very mean of Science

To go and interfere!
I slew a worm the other day —
A "Savant" passing by
Murmured "Resurgam" — "Centipede"!
"Oh Lord — how frail are we"!
I pull a flower from the woods —
A monster with a glass
Computes the stamens in a breath —
And has her in a "class"!
Whereas I took the Butterfly
Aforetime in my hat —
He sits erect in "Cabinets" —
The Clover bells forgot.
What once was "Heaven" is "Zenith" now —
Where I proposed to go
When Time's brief masquerade was done
Is mapped and charted too.
What if the poles should frisk about
And stand upon their heads!
I hope I'm ready for "the worst" —
Whatever prank betides!
Perhaps the "Kingdom of Heaven's" changed —
I hope the "Children" there
Won't be "new fashioned" when I come —
And laugh at me — and stare —
I hope the Father in the skies
Will lift his little girl —
Old fashioned — naught — everything —
Over the stile of "Pearl."

Safe in their Alabaster Chambers —
Untouched by Morning
And untouched by Noon —
Sleep the meek members of the Resurrection —
Rafter of satin,
And Roof of stone.

Light laughs the breeze
In her Castle above them —
Babbles the Bee in a stolid Ear,
Pipe the Sweet Birds in ignorant cadence —
Ah, what sagacity perished here!

Grand go the years in the crescent above them;
Worlds scoop their arcs, and firmaments row,
Diadems drop and Doges surrender,
Soundless as dots on a disk of snow.

Who never lost, are unprepared
A Coronet to find!
Who never thirsted
Flagons, and Cooling Tamarind!

Who never climbed the weary league —
Can such a foot explore
The purple territories
On Pizarro's shore?

How many Legions overcome —
The Emperor will say?
How many Colors taken
On Revolution Day?

How many Bullets bearest?
Hast Thou the Royal scar?
Angels! Write "Promoted"
On this Soldier's brow!

⁓

"Houses" — so the Wise Men tell me —
"Mansions"! Mansions must be warm!
Mansions cannot let the tears in,
Mansions must exclude the storm!

"Many Mansions," by "his Father,"
I don't know him; snugly built!
Could the Children find the way there —
Some, would even trudge tonight!

A science — so the Savants say,
"Comparative Anatomy" —
By which a single bone —
Is made a secret to unfold
Of some rare tenant of the mold,
Else perished in the stone —

So to the eye prospective led,
This meekest flower of the mead
Upon a winter's day,
Stands representative in gold
Of Rose and Lily, manifold,
And countless Butterfly!

'Twas such a little — little boat
That toddled down the bay!
'Twas such a gallant — gallant sea
That beckoned it away!

'Twas such a greedy, greedy wave
That licked it from the Coast —

Nor ever guessed the stately sails
My little craft was lost!

෴

Where I have lost, I softer tread —
I sow sweet flower from garden bed —
I pause above that vanished head
And mourn.

Whom I have lost, I pious guard
From accent harsh, or ruthless word —
Feeling as if their pillow heard,
Though stone!

When I have lost, you'll know by this —
A Bonnet black — A dusk surplice —
A little tremor in my voice
Like this!

Why, I have lost, the people know
Who dressed in flocks of purest snow
Went home a century ago
Next Bliss!

෴

The daisy follows soft the sun,
And when his golden walk is done,
    Sits shyly at his feet.
He, walking, finds the flower near.
"Wherefore, marauder, art thou here?
    "Because, sir, love is sweet!"

We are the flower, Thou the sun!
Forgive us, if as days decline,
    We nearer steal to Thee, —
Enamoured of the parting west,
The peace, the flight, the amethyst,
    Night's possibility!

ᴄᴐ

A fuzzy fellow, without feet,
Yet doth exceeding run!
Of velvet, is his Countenance,
And his Complexion, dun!

Sometime, he dwelleth in the grass!
Sometime, upon a bough,
From which he doth descend in plush
Upon the Passer-by!

All this in summer.

But when winds alarm the Forest Folk,
He taketh Damask Residence —
And struts in sewing silk!

Then, finer than a Lady,
Emerges in the spring!
A Feather on each shoulder!
You'd scarce recognize him!

By Men, yclept Caterpillar!
By me! But who am I,
To tell the pretty secret
Of the Butterfly!

☙

A wounded deer leaps highest,
I've heard the hunter tell;
'T is but the ecstasy of death,
And then the brake is still.

The smitten rock that gushes,
The trampled steel that springs:
A cheek is always redder
Just where the hectic stings!

Mirth is the mail of anguish,
In which it cautions arm,

Lest anybody spy the blood
And "You're hurt" exclaim!

❧

The Rose did caper on her cheek —
Her Bodice rose and fell —
Her pretty speech — like drunken men —
Did stagger pitiful —

Her fingers fumbled at her work —
Her needle would not go —
What ailed so smart a little Maid —
It puzzled me to know —

Till opposite — I spied a cheek
That bore another Rose —
Just opposite — Another speech
That like the Drunkard goes —

A Vest that like her Bodice, danced —
To the immortal tune —
Till those two troubled — little Clocks
Ticked softly into one.

❧

Come slowly — Eden!
Lips unused to Thee —
Bashful — sip they Jessamines —
as the fainting Bee —
Reaching late his flower,
Round her chamber hums —
Counts his nectars —
Enters — and is lost in Balms.

ᕙᕗ

I taste a liquor never brewed,
From tankards scooped in pearl;
Not all the vats upon the Rhine
Yield such an alcohol!

Inebriate of air am I,
And debauchee of dew,
Reeling, through endless summer days,
From inns of molten blue.

When landlords turn the drunken bee
Out of the foxglove's door,
When butterflies renounce their drams,
I shall but drink the more!

Till seraphs swing their snowy hats,
And saints to windows run,

To see the little tippler
Leaning against the sun!

           ~∽

A feather from the Whippowill
That everlasting — sings!
Whose galleries — are Sunrise —
Whose Opera — the Springs —
Whose Emerald Nest the Ages spin
Of mellow — murmuring thread —
Whose Beryl Egg, what Schoolboys hunt
In "Recess" — Overhead!

           ~∽

I shall know why, when time is over,
And I have ceased to wonder why;
Christ will explain each separate anguish
In the fair schoolroom of the sky.

He will tell me what Peter promised,
And I, for wonder at his woe,
I shall forget the drop of anguish
That scalds me now, that scalds me now.

My River runs to thee —
Blue Sea! Wilt welcome me?
My River waits reply —
Oh Sea — look graciously —
I'll fetch thee Brooks
From spotted nooks —
Say — Sea — Take Me!

Dying! Dying in the night!
Won't somebody bring the light
So I can see which way to go
Into the everlasting snow?

And "Jesus"! Where is Jesus gone?
They said that Jesus — always came —
Perhaps he doesn't know the House —
This way, Jesus, Let him pass!

Somebody run to the great gate
And see if Dollie's coming! Wait!
I hear her feet upon the stair!
Death won't hurt — now Dollie's here!

Musicians wrestle everywhere —
All day — among the crowded air
I hear the silver strife —
And — waking — long before the morn —
Such transport breaks upon the town
I think it that "New Life"!

It is not Bird — it has no nest —
Nor "Band" — in brass and scarlet — drest —
Nor Tamborin — nor Man —
It is not Hymn from pulpit read —
The "Morning Stars" the Treble led
On Time's first Afternoon!

Some — say — it is "the Spheres" — at play!
Some say that bright Majority
Of vanished Dames — and Men!
Some — think it service in the place
Where we — with late — celestial face —
Please God — shall Ascertain!

A slash of Blue —
A sweep of Gray —
Some scarlet patches on the way,
Compose an Evening Sky —
A little purple — slipped between —
Some Ruby Trousers hurried on —
A Wave of Gold —
A Bank of Day —
This just makes out the Morning Sky.

ℂσ

Make me a picture of the sun —
So I can hang it in my room —
And make believe I'm getting warm
When others call it "Day"!

Draw me a Robin — on a stem —
So I am hearing him, I'll dream,
And when the Orchards stop their tune —
Put my pretense — away —

Say if it's really — warm at noon —
Whether it's Buttercups — that "skim" —
Or Butterflies — that "bloom"?
Then — skip — the frost — upon the lea —
And skip the Russet — on the tree —
Let's play those — never come!

What is — "Paradise" —
Who live there —
Are they "Farmers" —
Do they "hoe" —
Do they know that this is "Amherst" —
And that I — am coming — too —

Do they wear "new shoes" — in "Eden" —
Is it always pleasant — there —
Won't they scold us — when we're homesick —
Or tell God — how cross we are —

You are sure there's such a person
As "a Father" — in the sky —
So if I get lost — there — ever —
Or do what the Nurse calls "die" —
I shan't walk the "Jasper" — barefoot —
Ransomed folks — won't laugh at me —
Maybe — "Eden" a'n't so lonesome
As New England used to be!

You're right — "the way is narrow" —
And "difficult the Gate" —
And "few there be" — Correct again —
That "enter in — thereat" —

'Tis Costly — So are purples!
'Tis just the price of Breath —
With but the "Discount" of the Grave —
Termed by the Brokers — "Death"!

And after that — there's Heaven —
The Good Man's — "Dividend" —
And Bad Men — "go to Jail" —
I guess —

∾

The Drop, that wrestles in the Sea —
Forgets her own locality —
As I — toward Thee —

She knows herself an incense small —
Yet small — she sighs — if All — is All —
How larger — be?

The Ocean — smiles — at her Conceit —
But she, forgetting Amphitrite —
Pleads — "Me"?

∽

I Came to buy a smile — today —
But just a single smile —
The smallest one upon your face
Will suit me just as well —
The one that no one else would miss
It shone so very small —
I'm pleading at the "counter" — sir —
Could you afford to sell —
I've Diamonds — on my fingers —
You know what Diamonds are?
I've Rubies — live the Evening Blood —
And Topaz — like the star!
'Twould be "a Bargain" for a Jew!
Say — may I have it — Sir?

∽

I held a Jewel in my fingers —
And went to sleep —
The day was warm, and winds were prosy —
I said "'Twill keep" —

I woke — and chid my honest fingers,
The Gem was gone —

And now, an Amethyst remembrance
Is all I own —

cso

It can't be "Summer"!
That — got through!
It's early — yet — for "Spring"!
There's that long town of White — to cross —
Before the Blackbirds sing!
It can't be "Dying"!
It's too Rouge —
The Dead shall go in White —
So Sunset shuts my question down
With Cuffs of Chrysolite!

cso

Wild Nights — Wild Nights!
Were I with thee
Wild Nights should be
Our luxury!

Futile — the Winds —
To a Heart in port —

Done with the Compass —
Done with the Chart!

Rowing in Eden —
Ah, the Sea!
Might I but moor — Tonight —
In Thee!

❧

Over the fence —
Strawberries — grow —
Over the fence —
I could climb — if I tried, I know —
Berries are nice!

But — if I stained my Apron —
God would certainly scold!
Oh, dear, — I guess if He were a Boy —
He'd — climb — if He could!

❧

Again — his voice is at the door —
I feel the old Degree —

I hear him ask the servant
For such an one — as me —

I take a flower — as I go —
My face to justify —
He never saw me — in this life —
I might surprise his eye!

I cross the Hall with mingled steps —
I — silent — pass the door —
I look on all this world contains —
Just his face — nothing more!

We talk in careless — and it toss —
A kind of plummet strain —
Each — sounding — shyly —
Just — how — deep —
The other's one — had been —

We walk — I leave my Dog — at home —
A tender — thoughtful Moon —
Goes with us — just a little way —
And — then — we are alone —

Alone — if Angels are "alone" —
First time they try the sky!
Alone — if those "veiled faces" — be —
We cannot count — on High!

I'd give — to live that hour — again —
The purple — in my Vein —

But He must count the drops — himself —
My price for every stain!

⌒

Of all the Souls that stand create —
I have elected — One —
When Sense from Spirit — files away —
And Subterfuge — is done —
When that which is — and that which was —
Apart — intrinsic — stand —
And this brief Drama in the flesh —
Is shifted — like a Sand —
When Figures show their royal Front —
And Mists — are carved away,
Behold the Atom — I preferred —
To all the lists of Clay!

⌒

I should have been too glad, I see —
Too lifted — for the scant degree
Of Life's penurious Round —
My little Circuit would have shamed

This new Circumference — have blamed —
The homelier time behind.

I should have been too saved — I see —
Too rescued — Fear too dim to me
That I could spell the Prayer
I knew so perfect — yesterday —
That Scalding One — Sabachthani —
Recited fluent — here —

Earth would have been too much — I see —
And Heaven — not enough for me —
I should have had the Joy
Without the Fear — to justify —
The Palm — without the Calvary —
So Savior — Crucify —
Defeat — whets Victory — they say —
The Reefs — in old Gethsemane —
Endear the Coast — beyond!
'Tis Beggars — Banquets — can define —
'Tis Parching — vitalizes Wine —
"Faith" bleats — to understand!

ᏊᎾ

The Love a Life can show Below
Is but a filament, I know,
Of that diviner thing

That faints upon the face of Noon —
And smites the Tinder in the Sun —
And hinders Gabriel's Wing —

'Tis this — in Music — hints and sways —
And far abroad on Summer days —
Distils uncertain pain —
'Tis this enamors in the East —
And tints the Transit in the West
With harrowing Iodine —

'Tis this — invites — appalls — endows —
Flits — glimmers — proves — dissolves —
Returns — suggests — convicts — enchants —
Then — flings in Paradise —

ᕤ

It sifts from Leaden Sieves —
It powders all the Wood.
It fills with Alabaster Wool
The Wrinkles of the Road —

It makes an Even Face
Of Mountain, and of Plain —
Unbroken Forehead from the East
Unto the East again —

It reaches to the Fence —
It wraps it Rail by Rail
Till it is lost in Fleeces —
It deals Celestial Vail

To Stump, and Stack — and Stem —
A Summer's empty Room —
Acres of Joints, where Harvests were,
Recordless, but for them —

It Ruffles Wrists of Posts
As Ankles of a Queen —
Then stills its Artisans — like Ghosts —
Denying they have been —

~⌒~

Where Ships of Purple — gently toss —
On Seas of Daffodil —
Fantastic Sailors — mingle —
And then — the Wharf is still!

~⌒~

Unto like Story — Trouble has enticed me —
How Kinsmen fell —
Brothers and Sisters — who preferred the Glory —
And their young will
Bent to the Scaffold, or in Dungeons — chanted —
Till God's full time —
When they let go the ignominy — smiling —
And Shame went still —

Unto guessed Crests, my moaning fancy, leads me,
Worn fair
By Heads rejected — in the lower country —
Of honors there —
Such spirit makes her perpetual mention,
That I — grown bold —
Step martial — at my Crucifixion —
As Trumpets — rolled —

Feet, small as mine — have marched in Revolution
Firm to the Drum —
Hands — not so stout — hoisted them — in witness
—

When Speech went numb —
Let me not shame their sublime deportments —
Drilled bright —
Beckoning — Etruscan invitation —
Toward Light —

What if I say I shall not wait!
What if I burst the fleshly Gate —
And pass escaped — to thee!

What if I file this Mortal — off —
See where it hurt me — That's enough —
And wade in Liberty!

They cannot take me — any more!
Dungeons can call — and Guns implore
Unmeaning — now — to me —

As laughter — was — an hour ago —
Or Laces — or a Travelling Show —
Or who died — yesterday!

↭

A solemn thing — it was — I said —
A woman — white — to be —
And wear — if God should count me fit —
Her blameless mystery —

A hallowed thing — to drop a life
Into the purple well —
Too plummetless — that it return —
Eternity — until —

I pondered how the bliss would look —
And would it feel as big —
When I could take it in my hand —
As hovering — seen — through fog —

And then — the size of this "small" life —
The Sages — call it small —
Swelled — like Horizons — in my vest —
And I sneered — softly — "small"!

ᥴᡂ

"Hope" is the thing with feathers
That perches in the soul
And sings the tune without the words
And never stops at all

And sweetest in the Gale is heard
And sore must be the storm —
That could abash the little Bird
That kept so many warm —

I've heard it in the chillest land —
And on the strangest Sea —
Yet, never, in Extremity,
It asked a crumb — of Me.

Of Bronze — and Blaze —
The North — Tonight —
So adequate — it forms —
So preconcerted with itself —
So distant — to alarms —
An Unconcern so sovereign
To Universe, or me —
Infects my simple spirit
With Taints of Majesty —
Till I take vaster attitudes —
And strut upon my stem —
Disdaining Men, and Oxygen,
For Arrogance of them —

My Splendors, are Menagerie —
But their Competeless Show
Will entertain the Centuries
When I, am long ago,
An Island in dishonored Grass —
Whom none but Beetles — know.

Blazing in Gold and quenching in Purple
Leaping like Leopards to the Sky
Then at the feet of the old Horizon
Laying her spotted Face to die
Stooping as low as the Otter's Window
Touching the Roof and tinting the Barn
Kissing her Bonnet to the Meadow
And the Juggler of Day is gone

There came a Day at Summer's full,
Entirely for me —
I thought that such were for the Saints,
Where Resurrections — be —

The Sun, as common, went abroad,
The flowers, accustomed, blew,
As if no soul the solstice passed
That maketh all things new —

The time was scarce profaned, by speech —
The symbol of a word
Was needless, as at Sacrament,
The Wardrobe — of our Lord —

Each was to each The Sealed Church,
Permitted to commune this — time —

Lest we too awkward show
At Supper of the Lamb.

The Hours slid fast — as Hours will,
Clutched tight, by greedy hands —
So faces on two Decks, look back,
Bound to opposing lands —

And so when all the time had leaked,
Without external sound
Each bound the Other's Crucifix —
We gave no other Bond —

Sufficient troth, that we shall rise —
Deposed — at length, the Grave —
To that new Marriage,
Justified — through Calvaries of Love —

ᕯ

If your Nerve, deny you —
Go above your Nerve —
He can lean against the Grave,
If he fear to swerve —

That's a steady posture —
Never any bend
Held of those Brass arms —
Best Giant made —

If your Soul seesaw —
Lift the Flesh door —
The Poltroon wants Oxygen —
Nothing more —

೧

Many a phrase has the English language —
I have heard but one —
Low as the laughter of the Cricket,
Loud, as the Thunder's Tongue —

Murmuring, like old Caspian Choirs,
When the Tide's a' lull —
Saying itself in new infection —
Like a Whippoorwill —

Breaking in bright Orthography
On my simple sleep —
Thundering its Prospective —
Till I stir, and weep —

Not for the Sorrow, done me —
But the push of Joy —
Say it again, Saxon!
Hush — Only to me!

I would not paint — a picture —
I'd rather be the One
Its bright impossibility
To dwell — delicious — on —
And wonder how the fingers feel
Whose rare — celestial — stir —
Evokes so sweet a Torment —
Such sumptuous — Despair —

I would not talk, like Cornets —
I'd rather be the One
Raised softly to the Ceilings —
And out, and easy on —
Through Villages of Ether —
Myself endued Balloon
By but a lip of Metal —
The pier to my Pontoon —

Nor would I be a Poet —
It's finer — own the Ear —
Enamored — impotent — content —
The License to revere,
A privilege so awful
What would the Dower be,
Had I the Art to stun myself
With Bolts of Melody!

If anybody's friend be dead
It's sharpest of the theme
The thinking how they walked alive —
At such and such a time —

Their costume, of a Sunday,
Some manner of the Hair —
A prank nobody knew but them
Lost, in the Sepulchre —

How warm, they were, on such a day,
You almost feel the date —
So short way off it seems —
And now — they're Centuries from that —

How pleased they were, at what you said —
You try to touch the smile
And dip your fingers in the frost —
When was it — Can you tell —

You asked the Company to tea —
Acquaintance — just a few —
And chatted close with this Grand Thing
That don't remember you —

Past Bows, and Invitations —
Past Interview, and Vow —

Past what Ourself can estimate —
That — makes the Quick of Woe!

∽

I know a place where Summer strives
With such a practised Frost —
She — each year — leads her Daisies back —
Recording briefly — "Lost" —

But when the South Wind stirs the Pools
And struggles in the lanes —
Her Heart misgives Her, for Her Vow —
And she pours soft Refrains

Into the lap of Adamant —
And spices — and the Dew —
That stiffens quietly to Quartz —
Upon her Amber Shoe —

∽

I envy Seas, whereon He rides —
I envy Spokes of Wheels
Of Chariots, that Him convey —
I envy Crooked Hills

That gaze upon His journey —
How easy All can see
What is forbidden utterly
As Heaven — unto me!

I envy Nests of Sparrows —
That dot His distant Eaves —
The wealthy Fly, upon His Pane —
The happy — happy Leaves —

That just abroad His Window
Have Summer's leave to play —
The Ear Rings of Pizarro
Could not obtain for me —

I envy Light — that wakes Him —
And Bells — that boldly ring
To tell Him it is Noon, abroad —
Myself — be Noon to Him —

Yet interdict — my Blossom —
And abrogate — my Bee —
Lest Noon in Everlasting Night —
Drop Gabriel — and Me —

ᥫᩚ

At least — to pray — is left — is left —
Oh Jesus — in the Air —
I know not which thy chamber is —
I'm knocking — everywhere —

Thou settest Earthquake in the South —
And Maelstrom, in the Sea —
Say, Jesus Christ of Nazareth —
Hast thou no Arm for Me?

☙

Good Morning — Midnight —
I'm coming Home —
Day — got tired of Me —
How could I — of Him?

Sunshine was a sweet place —
I liked to stay —
But Morn — didn't want me — now —
So — Goodnight — Day!

I can look — can't I —
When the East is Red?
The Hills — have a way — then —
That puts the Heart — abroad —

You — are not so fair — Midnight —
I chose — Day —
But — please take a little Girl —
He turned away!

∽

The Moon is distant from the Sea —
And yet, with Amber Hands —
She leads Him — docile as a Boy —
Along appointed Sands —

He never misses a Degree —
Obedient to Her Eye
He comes just so far — toward the Town —
Just so far — goes away —

Oh, Signor, Thine, the Amber Hand —
And mine — the distant Sea —
Obedient to the least command
Thine eye impose on me —

∽

We talked as Girls do —
Fond, and late —
We speculated fair, on every subject, but the Grave —
Of ours, none affair —

We handled Destinies, as cool —
As we — Disposers — be —
And God, a Quiet Party
To our Authority —

But fondest, dwelt upon Ourself
As we eventual — be —
When Girls to Women, softly raised
We — occupy — Degree —

We parted with a contract
To cherish, and to write
But Heaven made both, impossible
Before another night.

୨

To hear an Oriole sing
May be a common thing —
Or only a divine.

It is not of the Bird
Who sings the same, unheard,
As unto Crowd —

The Fashion of the Ear
Attireth that it hear
In Dun, or fair —

So whether it be Rune,
Or whether it be none
Is of within.

The "Tune is in the Tree —"
The Skeptic — showeth me —
"No Sir! In Thee!"

ᘖ

One need not be a Chamber — to be Haunted —
One need not be a House —
The Brain has Corridors — surpassing
Material Place —

Far safer, of a Midnight Meeting
External Ghost
Than its interior Confronting —
That Cooler Host.

Far safer, through an Abbey gallop,
The Stones a'chase —
Than Unarmed, one's a'self encounter —
In lonesome Place —

Ourself behind ourself, concealed —
Should startle most —
Assassin hid in our Apartment
Be Horror's least.

The Body — borrows a Revolver —
He bolts the Door —
O'erlooking a superior spectre —
Or More —

༺

The Months have ends — the Years — a knot —
No Power can untie
To stretch a little further
A Skein of Misery —

The Earth lays back these tired lives
In her mysterious Drawers —
Too tenderly, that any doubt
An ultimate Repose —

The manner of the Children —
Who weary of the Day —
Themself — the noisy Plaything
They cannot put away —

&

The first Day's Night had come —
And grateful that a thing
So terrible — had been endured —
I told my Soul to sing —

She said her Strings were snapt —
Her Bow — to Atoms blown —
And so to mend her — gave me work
Until another Morn —

And then — a Day as huge
As Yesterdays in pairs,
Unrolled its horror in my face —
Until it blocked my eyes —

My Brain — begun to laugh —
I mumbled — like a fool —
And tho' 'tis Years ago — that Day —
My Brain keeps giggling — still.

And Something's odd — within —

That person that I was —
And this One — do not feel the same —
Could it be Madness — this?

⌒

We grow accustomed to the Dark —
When light is put away —
As when the Neighbor holds the Lamp
To witness her Goodbye —

A Moment — We uncertain step
For newness of the night —
Then — fit our Vision to the Dark —
And meet the Road — erect —

And so of larger — Darkness —
Those Evenings of the Brain —
When not a Moon disclose a sign —
Or Star — come out — within —

The Bravest — grope a little —
And sometimes hit a Tree
Directly in the Forehead —
But as they learn to see —

Either the Darkness alters —
Or something in the sight

Adjusts itself to Midnight —
And Life steps almost straight.

∽

Not in this World to see his face —
Sounds long — until I read the place
Where this — is said to be
But just the Primer — to a life —
Unopened — rare — Upon the Shelf —
Clasped yet — to Him — and Me —

And yet — My Primer suits me so
I would not choose — a Book to know
Than that — be sweeter wise —
Might some one else — so learned — be —
And leave me — just my A — B — C —
Himself — could have the Skies —

∽

I Years had been from Home
And now before the Door
I dared not enter, lest a Face
I never saw before

Stare solid into mine
And ask my Business there —
"My Business but a Life I left
Was such remaining there?"

I leaned upon the Awe —
I lingered with Before —
The Second like an Ocean rolled
And broke against my ear —

I laughed a crumbling Laugh
That I could fear a Door
Who Consternation compassed
And never winced before.

I fitted to the Latch
My Hand, with trembling care
Lest back the awful Door should spring
And leave me in the Floor —

Then moved my Fingers off
As cautiously as Glass
And held my ears, and like a Thief
Fled gasping from the House —

They shut me up in Prose —
As when a little Girl
They put me in the Closet —
Because they liked me "still" —

Still! Could themself have peeped —
And seen my Brain — go round —
They might as wise have lodged a Bird
For Treason — in the Pound —

Himself has but to will
And easy as a Star
Abolish his Captivity —
And laugh — No more have I —

I died for beauty, but was scarce
Adjusted in the tomb,
When one who died for truth was lain
In an adjoining room.

He questioned softly why I failed?
"For beauty," I replied.
"And I for truth, — the two are one ;
We brethren are," he said.

And so, as kinsmen met a night,

We talked between the rooms,
Until the moss had reached our lips,
And covered up our names.

⤳

She dealt her pretty words like Blades —
How glittering they shone —
And every One unbared a Nerve
Or wantoned with a Bone —

She never deemed — she hurt —
That — is not Steel's Affair —
A vulgar grimace in the Flesh —
How ill the Creatures bear —

To Ache is human — not polite —
The Film upon the eye
Mortality's old Custom —
Just locking up — to Die.

⤳

"Why do I love" You, Sir?
Because —

The Wind does not require the Grass
To answer — Wherefore when He pass
She cannot keep Her place.

Because He knows — and
Do not You —
And We know not —
Enough for Us
The Wisdom it be so —

The Lightning — never asked an Eye
Wherefore it shut — when He was by —
Because He knows it cannot speak —
And reasons not contained —
— Of Talk —
There be — preferred by Daintier Folk —

The Sunrise — Sire — compelleth Me —
Because He's Sunrise — and I see —
Therefore — Then —
I love Thee —

ᴄᴏ

I dwell in Possibility —
A fairer House than Prose —
More numerous of Windows —
Superior — for Doors —

Of Chambers as the Cedars —
Impregnable of Eye —
And for an Everlasting Roof
The Gambrels of the Sky —

Of Visitors — the fairest —
For Occupation — This —
The spreading wide my narrow Hands
To gather Paradise —

ᥴ᥆

Because I could not stop for Death —
He kindly stopped for me —
The Carriage held but just Ourselves —
And Immortality.

We slowly drove — He knew no haste,
And I had put away
My labor and my leisure too,
For His Civility —

We passed the School, where Children strove
At recess — in the ring —
We passed the Fields of Gazing Grain —
We passed the Setting Sun —

Or rather — He passed Us —
The Dews drew quivering and chill —
For only Gossamer, my Gown —
My Tippet — only Tulle —

We paused before a House that seemed
A Swelling of the Ground —
The Roof was scarcely visible —
The Cornice — in the Ground —

Since then — 'tis centuries — and yet
Feels shorter than the Day
I first surmised the Horses' Heads
Were toward Eternity —

ഗ

From Blank to Blank —
A Threadless Way
I pushed Mechanic feet —
To stop — or perish — or advance —
Alike indifferent —

If end I gained
It ends beyond
Indefinite disclosed —
I shut my eyes — and groped as well
'Twas lighter — to be Blind —

Rest at Night
The Sun from shining,
Nature — and some Men —
Rest at Noon — some Men —
While Nature
And the Sun — go on —

To offer brave assistance
To Lives that stand alone —
When One has failed to stop them —
Is Human — but Divine

To lend an Ample Sinew
Unto a Nameless Man —
Whose Homely Benediction
No other — stopped to earn —

The Wind didn't come from the Orchard — today —
Further than that —
Nor stop to play with the Hay —
Nor joggle a Hat —
He's a transitive fellow — very —
Rely on that —

If He leave a Bur at the door
We know He has climbed a Fir —
But the Fir is Where — Declare —
Were you ever there?

If He brings Odors of Clovers —
And that is His business — not Ours —
Then He has been with the Mowers —
Whetting away the Hours
To sweet pauses of Hay —
His Way — of a June Day —

If He fling Sand, and Pebble —
Little Boys Hats — and Stubble —
With an occasional Steeple —
And a hoarse "Get out of the way, I say,"
Who'd be the fool to stay?
Would you — Say —
Would you be the fool to stay?

ഗ

Light is sufficient to itself —
If Others want to see
It can be had on Window Panes
Some Hours in the Day.

But not for Compensation —
It holds as large a Glow
To Squirrel in the Himmaleh
Precisely, as to you.

A curious Cloud surprised the Sky,
'Twas like a sheet with Horns;
The sheet was Blue —
The Antlers Gray —
It almost touched the lawns.

So low it leaned — then statelier drew —
And trailed like robes away,
A Queen adown a satin aisle
Had not the majesty.

The Spider holds a Silver Ball
In unperceived Hands —
And dancing softly to Himself
His Yarn of Pearl — unwinds —

He plies from Nought to Nought —
In unsubstantial Trade —
Supplants our Tapestries with His —
In half the period —

An Hour to rear supreme
His Continents of Light —
Then dangle from the Housewife's Broom —
His Boundaries — forgot —

This is my letter to the World
That never wrote to Me —
The simple News that Nature told —
With tender Majesty

Her Message is committed
To Hands I cannot see —
For love of Her — Sweet — countrymen —
Judge tenderly — of Me

A Dying Tiger — moaned for Drink —
I hunted all the Sand —
I caught the Dripping of a Rock
And bore it in my Hand —

His Mighty Balls — in death were thick —
But searching — I could see
A Vision on the Retina
Of Water — and of me —

'Twas not my blame — who sped too slow —
'Twas not his blame — who died
While I was reaching him —
But 'twas — the fact that He was dead —

We learned the Whole of Love —
The Alphabet — the Words —
A Chapter — then the mighty Book —
Then — Revelation closed —

But in Each Other's eyes
An Ignorance beheld —

Diviner than the Childhood's —
And each to each, a Child —

Attempted to expound
What Neither — understood —
Alas, that Wisdom is so large —
And Truth — so manifold!

ᘓ

The Test of Love — is Death —
Our Lord — "so loved" — it saith —
What Largest Lover — hath
Another — doth —

If smaller Patience — be —
Through less Infinity —
If Bravo, sometimes swerve —
Through fainter Nerve —

Accept its Most —
And overlook — the Dust —
Last — Least —
The Cross' — Request —

ᘓ

The Black Berry — wears a Thorn in his side —
But no Man heard Him cry —
He offers His Berry, just the same
To Partridge — and to Boy —

He sometimes holds upon the Fence —
Or struggles to a Tree —
Or clasps a Rock, with both His Hands —
But not for Sympathy —

We — tell a Hurt — to cool it —
This Mourner — to the Sky
A little further reaches — instead —
Brave Black Berry —

c∽

I measure every Grief I meet
With narrow, probing, Eyes —
I wonder if It weighs like Mine —
Or has an Easier size.

I wonder if They bore it long —
Or did it just begin —
I could not tell the Date of Mine —
It feels so old a pain —

I wonder if it hurts to live —
And if They have to try —
And whether — could They choose between —
It would not be — to die —

I note that Some — gone patient long —
At length, renew their smile —
An imitation of a Light
That has so little Oil —

I wonder if when Years have piled —
Some Thousands — on the Harm —
That hurt them early — such a lapse   .
Could give them any Balm —

Or would they go on aching still
Through Centuries of Nerve —
Enlightened to a larger Pain —
In Contrast with the Love —

The Grieved — are many — I am told —
There is the various Cause —
Death — is but one — and comes but once —
And only nails the eyes —

There's Grief of Want — and Grief of Cold —
A sort they call "Despair" —
There's Banishment from native Eyes —
In sight of Native Air —

And though I may not guess the kind —
Correctly — yet to me
A piercing Comfort it affords
In passing Calvary —

To note the fashions — of the Cross —
And how they're mostly worn —
Still fascinated to presume
That Some — are like My Own —

When Diamonds are a Legend,
And Diadems — a Tale —
I Brooch and Earrings for Myself,
Do sow, and Raise for sale —

And tho' I'm scarce accounted,
My Art, a Summer Day — had Patrons —
Once — it was a Queen —
And once — a Butterfly. —

⤳

I send Two Sunsets —
Day and I — in competition ran —
I finished Two — and several Stars —
While He — was making One —

His own was ampler — but as I
Was saying to a friend —
Mine — is the more convenient
To Carry in the Hand —

Trust in the Unexpected —
By this — was William Kidd
Persuaded of the Buried Gold —
As One had testified —

Through this — the old Philosopher —
His Talismanic Stone
Discerned — still withholden
To effort undivine —

'Twas this — allured Columbus —
When Genoa — withdrew
Before an Apparition
Baptized America —

The Same — afflicted Thomas —
When Deity assured
'Twas better — the perceiving not —
Provided it believed —

cᴚ

Two butterflies went out at Noon —
And waltzed upon a Farm —
Then stepped straight through the Firmament
And rested, on a Beam —

And then — together bore away
Upon a shining Sea —
Though never yet, in any Port —
Their coming, mentioned — be —

If spoken by the distant Bird —
If met in Ether Sea
By Frigate, or by Merchantman —
No notice — was — to me —

cᴚ

The Day came slow — till Five o'clock —
Then sprang before the Hills
Like Hindered Rubies — or the Light
A Sudden Musket — spills —

The Purple could not keep the East —
The Sunrise shook abroad

Like Breadths of Topaz — packed a Night —
The Lady just unrolled —

The Happy Winds — their Timbrels took —
The Birds — in docile Rows
Arranged themselves around their Prince
The Wind — is Prince of Those —

The Orchard sparkled like a Jew —
How mighty 'twas — to be
A Guest in this stupendous place —
The Parlor — of the Day —

౭

The Angle of a Landscape —
That every time I wake —
Between my Curtain and the Wall
Upon an ample Crack —

Like a Venetian — waiting —
Accosts my open eye —
Is just a Bough of Apples —
Held slanting, in the Sky —

The Pattern of a Chimney —
The Forehead of a Hill —

Sometimes — a Vane's Forefinger —
But that's — Occasional —

The Seasons — shift — my Picture —
Upon my Emerald Bough,
I wake — to find no — Emeralds —
Then — Diamonds — which the Snow

From Polar Caskets — fetched me —
The Chimney — and the Hill —
And just the Steeple's finger —
These — never stir at all —

ᖇ

You cannot put a Fire out —
A Thing that can ignite
Can go, itself, without a Fan —
Upon the slowest Night —

You cannot fold a Flood —
And put it in a Drawer —
Because the Winds would find it out —
And tell your Cedar Floor —

ᖇ

The Lightning playeth — all the while —
But when He singeth — then —
Ourselves are conscious He exist —
And we approach Him — stern —

With Insulators — and a Glove —
Whose short — sepulchral Bass
Alarms us — tho' His Yellow feet
May pass — and counterpass —

Upon the Ropes — above our Head —
Continual — with the News —
Nor We so much as check our speech —
Nor stop to cross Ourselves —

⌒

The Manner of its Death
When Certain it must die —
'Tis deemed a privilege to choose —
'Twas Major Andre's Way —

When Choice of Life — is past —
There yet remains a Love
Its little Fate to stipulate —

How small in those who live —

The Miracle to tease
With Bable of the styles —
How "they are Dying mostly — now" —
And Customs at "St. James"!

⌁

I think the longest Hour of all
Is when the Cars have come —
And we are waiting for the Coach —
It seems as though the Time

Indignant — that the Joy was come —
Did block the Gilded Hands —
And would not let the Seconds by —
But slowest instant — ends —

The Pendulum begins to count —
Like little Scholars — loud —
The steps grow thicker — in the Hall —
The Heart begins to crowd —

Then I — my timid service done —
Tho' service 'twas, of Love —
Take up my little Violin —
And further North — remove.

Her sweet Weight on my Heart a Night
Had scarcely deigned to lie —
When, stirring, for Belief's delight,
My Bride had slipped away —

If 'twas a Dream — made solid — just
The Heaven to confirm —
Or if Myself were dreamed of Her —
The power to presume —

With Him remain — who unto Me —
Gave — even as to All —
A Fiction superseding Faith —
By so much — as 'twas real —

The Night was wide, and furnished scant
With but a single Star —
That often as a Cloud it met —
Blew out itself — for fear —

The Wind pursued the little Bush —
And drove away the Leaves

November left — then clambered up
And fretted in the Eaves —

No Squirrel went abroad —
A Dog's belated feet
Like intermittent Plush, be heard
Adown the empty Street —

To feel if Blinds be fast —
And closer to the fire —
Her little Rocking Chair to draw —
And shiver for the Poor —

The Housewife's gentle Task —
How pleasanter — said she
Unto the Sofa opposite —
The Sleet — than May, no Thee —

∽

Much madness is divinest sense
To a discerning eye;
Much sense the starkest madness.
'Tis the majority
In this, as all, prevails.
Assent, and you are sane;
Demur, — you're straightway dangerous,
And handled with a chain.

The Wind — tapped like a tired Man —
And like a Host — "Come in"
I boldly answered — entered then
My Residence within

A Rapid — footless Guest —
To offer whom a Chair
Were as impossible as hand
A Sofa to the Air —

No Bone had He to bind Him —
His Speech was like the Push
Of numerous Humming Birds at once
From a superior Bush —

His Countenance — a Billow —
His Fingers, as He passed
Let go a music — as of tunes
Blown tremulous in Glass —

He visited — still flitting —
Then like a timid Man
Again, He tapped — 'twas flurriedly —
And I became alone —

I think I was enchanted
When first a sombre Girl —
I read that Foreign Lady —
The Dark — felt beautiful —

And whether it was noon at night —
Or only Heaven — at Noon —
For very Lunacy of Light
I had not power to tell —

The Bees — became as Butterflies —
The Butterflies — as Swans —
Approached — and spurned the narrow Grass —
And just the meanest Tunes

That Nature murmured to herself
To keep herself in Cheer —
I took for Giants — practising
Titanic Opera —

The Days — to Mighty Metres stept —
The Homeliest — adorned
As if unto a Jubilee
'Twere suddenly Confirmed —

I could not have defined the change —
Conversion of the Mind
Like Sanctifying in the Soul —
Is Witnessed — not Explained —

'Twas a Divine Insanity —
The Danger to be sane
Should I again experience —
'Tis Antidote to turn —

To Tomes of solid Witchcraft —
Magicians be asleep —
But Magic — hath an Element —
Like Deity — to keep —

⁓

Sweet — You forgot — but I remembered
Every time — for Two —
So that the Sum be never hindered
Through Decay of You —

Say if I erred? Accuse my Farthings —
Blame the little Hand
Happy it be for You — a Beggar's —
Seeking More — to spend —

Just to be Rich — to waste my Guineas
On so Best a Heart —
Just to be Poor — for Barefoot Vision
You — Sweet — Shut me out —

A Secret told —
Ceases to be a Secret — then —
A Secret — kept —
That — can appal but One —

Better of it — continual be afraid —
Than it —
And Whom you told it to — beside —

Beauty — be not caused — It Is —
Chase it, and it ceases —
Chase it not, and it abides —

Overtake the Creases

In the Meadow — when the Wind
Runs his fingers thro' it —
Deity will see to it
That You never do it —

I took my Power in my Hand —
And went against the World —
'Twas not so much as David — had —
But I — was twice as bold —

I aimed by Pebble — but Myself
Was all the one that fell —
Was it Goliath — was too large —
Or was myself — too small?

∽

The Martyr Poets — did not tell —
But wrought their Pang in syllable —
That when their mortal name be numb —
Their mortal fate — encourage Some —

The Martyr Painters — never spoke —
Bequeathing — rather — to their Work —
That when their conscious fingers cease —
Some seek in Art — the Art of Peace —

∽

I could not prove the Years had feet —
Yet confident they run
Am I, from symptoms that are past
And Series that are done —

I find my feet have further Goals —
I smile upon the Aims
That felt so ample — Yesterday —
Today's — have vaster claims —

I do not doubt the self I was
Was competent to me —
But something awkward in the fit —
Proves that — outgrown — I see —

⁓

Funny — to be a Century —
And see the People — going by —
I — should die of the Oddity —
But then — I'm not so staid — as He —

He keeps His Secrets safely — very —
Were He to tell — extremely sorry
This Bashful Globe of Ours would be —
So dainty of Publicity —

Don't put up my Thread and Needle —
I'll begin to Sew
When the Birds begin to whistle —
Better Stitches — so —

These were bent — my sight got crooked —
When my mind — is plain
I'll do seams — a Queen's endeavor
Would not blush to own —

Hems — too fine for Lady's tracing
To the sightless Knot —
Tucks — of dainty interspersion —
Like a dotted Dot —

Leave my Needle in the furrow —
Where I put it down —
I can make the zigzag stitches
Straight — when I am strong —

Till then — dreaming I am sewing
Fetch the seam I missed —
Closer — so I — at my sleeping —
Still surmise I stitch —

Forever — is composed of Nows —
'Tis not a different time —
Except for Infiniteness —
And Latitude of Home —

From this — experienced Here —
Remove the Dates — to These —
Let Months dissolve in further Months —
And Years — exhale in Years —

Without Debate — or Pause —
Or Celebrated Days —
No different Our Years would be
From Anno Domini's —

ॐ

The power to be true to You,
Until upon my face
The Judgment push his Picture —
Presumptuous of Your Place —

Of This — Could Man deprive Me —
Himself — the Heaven excel —
Whose invitation — Yours reduced
Until it showed too small —

Doom is the House without the Door —
'Tis entered from the Sun —
And then the Ladder's thrown away,
Because Escape — is done —

'Tis varied by the Dream
Of what they do outside —
Where Squirrels play — and Berries die —
And Hemlocks — bow — to God —

The Sun kept setting — setting — still
No Hue of Afternoon —
Upon the Village I perceived
From House to House 'twas Noon —

The Dusk kept dropping — dropping — still
No Dew upon the Grass —
But only on my Forehead stopped —
And wandered in my Face —

My Feet kept drowsing — drowsing — still
My fingers were awake —

Yet why so little sound — Myself
Unto my Seeming — make?

How well I knew the Light before —
I could see it now —
'Tis Dying — I am doing — but
I'm not afraid to know —

I could bring You Jewels — had I a mind to —
But You have enough — of those —
I could bring You Odors from St. Domingo —
Colors — from Vera Cruz —

Berries of the Bahamas — have I —
But this little Blaze
Flickering to itself — in the Meadow —
Suits Me — more than those —

Never a Fellow matched this Topaz —
And his Emerald Swing —
Dower itself — for Bobadilo —
Better — Could I bring?

The Judge is like the Owl —
I've heard my Father tell —
And Owls do build in Oaks —
So here's an Amber Sill —

That slanted in my Path —
When going to the Barn —
And if it serve You for a House —
Itself is not in vain —

About the price — 'tis small —
I only ask a Tune
At Midnight — Let the Owl select
His favorite Refrain.

⤳

A Thought went up my mind today —
That I have had before —
But did not finish — some way back —
I could not fix the Year —

Nor where it went — nor why it came
The second time to me —
Nor definitely, what it was —
Have I the Art to say —

But somewhere — in my Soul — I know —
I've met the Thing before —
It just reminded me — 'twas all —
And came my way no more —

∞

Nature — the Gentlest Mother is,
Impatient of no Child —
The feeblest — or the waywardest —
Her Admonition mild —

In Forest — and the Hill —
By Traveller — be heard —
Restraining Rampant Squirrel —
Or too impetuous Bird —

How fair Her Conversation —
A Summer Afternoon —
Her Household — Her Assembly —
And when the Sun go down —

Her Voice among the Aisles
Incite the timid prayer
Of the minutest Cricket —
The most unworthy Flower —

When all the Children sleep —
She turns as long away

As will suffice to light Her lamps —
Then bending from the Sky —

With infinite Affection —
And infiniter Care —
Her Golden finger on Her lip —
Wills Silence — Everywhere —

༄

Sweet Mountains — Ye tell Me no lie —
Never deny Me — Never fly —
Those same unvarying Eyes
Turn on Me — when I fail — or feign,
Or take the Royal names in vain —
Their far — slow — Violet Gaze —

My Strong Madonnas — Cherish still —
The Wayward Nun — beneath the Hill —
Whose service — is to You —
Her latest Worship — When the Day
Fades from the Firmament away —
To lift Her Brows on You —

༄

Where Thou art — that — is Home —
Cashmere — or Calvary — the same —
Degree — or Shame —
I scarce esteem Location's Name —
So I may Come —

What Thou dost — is Delight —
Bondage as Play — be sweet —
Imprisonment — Content —
And Sentence — Sacrament —
Just We two — meet —

Where Thou art not — is Woe —
Tho' Bands of Spices — row —
What Thou dost not — Despair —
Tho' Gabriel — praise me — Sire —

⁓

Grief is a Mouse —
And chooses Wainscot in the Breast
For His Shy House —
And baffles quest —

Grief is a Thief — quick startled —
Pricks His Ear — report to hear
Of that Vast Dark —
That swept His Being — back —

Grief is a Juggler — boldest at the Play —
Lest if He flinch — the eye that way
Pounce on His Bruises — One — say — or Three —
Grief is a Gourmand — spare His luxury —

Best Grief is Tongueless — before He'll tell —
Burn Him in the Public Square —
His Ashes — will
Possibly — if they refuse — How then know —
Since a Rack couldn't coax a syllable — now.

∾

I had no time to Hate —
Because
The Grave would hinder Me —
And Life was not so
Ample I
Could finish — Enmity —

Nor had I time to Love —
But since
Some Industry must be —
The little Toil of Love —
I thought
Be large enough for Me —

My Life had stood — a Loaded Gun —
In Corners — till a Day
The Owner passed — identified —
And carried Me away —

And now We roam in Sovereign Woods —
And now We hunt the Doe —
And every time I speak for Him —
The Mountains straight reply —

And do I smile, such cordial light
Upon the Valley glow —
It is as a Vesuvian face
Had let its pleasure through —

And when at Night — Our good Day done —
I guard My Master's Head —
'Tis better than the Eider-Duck's
Deep Pillow — to have shared —

To foe of His — I'm deadly foe —
None stir the second time —
On whom I lay a Yellow Eye —
Or an emphatic Thumb —

Though I than He — may longer live
He longer must — than I —
For I have but the power to kill,
Without — the power to die —

❧

Never for Society
He shall seek in vain —
Who His own acquaintance
Cultivate — Of Men
Wiser Men may weary —
But the Man within

Never knew Satiety —
Better entertain
Than could Border Ballad —
Or Biscayan Hymn —
Neither introduction
Need You — unto Him —

❧

Drama's Vitallest Expression is the Common Day
That arise and set about Us —
Other Tragedy

Perish in the Recitation —
This — the best enact
When the Audience is scattered
And the Boxes shut —

"Hamlet" to Himself were Hamlet —
Had not Shakespeare wrote —
Though the "Romeo" left no Record
Of his Juliet,

It were infinite enacted
In the Human Heart —
Only Theatre recorded
Owner cannot shut —

⁓

Bloom upon the Mountain — stated —
Blameless of a Name —
Efflorescence of a Sunset —
Reproduced — the same —

Seed, had I, my Purple Sowing
Should endow the Day —
Not a Topic of a Twilight —
Show itself away —

Who for tilling — to the Mountain
Come, and disappear —
Whose be Her Renown, or fading,
Witness, is not here —

While I state — the Solemn Petals,
Far as North — and East,
Far as South and West — expanding —
Culminate — in Rest —

And the Mountain to the Evening
Fit His Countenance —
Indicating, by no Muscle —
The Experience —

∽

The Wind begun to knead the Grass —
As Women do a Dough —
He flung a Hand full at the Plain —
A Hand full at the Sky —
The Leaves unhooked themselves from Trees —
And started all abroad —
The Dust did scoop itself like Hands —
And throw away the Road —
The Wagons — quickened on the Street —
The Thunders gossiped low —
The Lightning showed a Yellow Head —

And then a livid Toe —
The Birds put up the Bars to Nests —
The Cattle flung to Barns —
Then came one drop of Giant Rain —
And then, as if the Hands
That held the Dams — had parted hold —
The Waters Wrecked the Sky —
But overlooked my Father's House —
Just Quartering a Tree —

As Sleigh Bells seem in summer
Or Bees, at Christmas show —
So fairy — so fictitious
The individuals do
Repealed from observation —
A Party that we knew —
More distant in an instant
Than Dawn in Timbuctoo.

The Robin for the Crumb
Returns no syllable

But long records the Lady's name
In Silver Chronicle.

⮑

This Consciousness that is aware
Of Neighbors and the Sun
Will be the one aware of Death
And that itself alone

Is traversing the interval
Experience between
And most profound experiment
Appointed unto Men —

How adequate unto itself
Its properties shall be
Itself unto itself and none
Shall make discovery —

Adventure most unto itself
The Soul condemned to be —
Attended by a single Hound
Its own identity.

⮑

The Admirations — and Contempts — of time —
Show justest — through an Open Tomb —
The Dying — as it were a Height

Reorganizes Estimate
And what We saw not
We distinguish clear —
And mostly — see not
What We saw before —

'Tis Compound Vision —
Light — enabling Light —
The Finite — furnished
With the Infinite —
Convex — and Concave Witness —
Back — toward Time —
And forward —
Toward the God of Him —

A Drop Fell on the Apple Tree —
Another — on the Roof —
A Half a Dozen kissed the Eaves —
And made the Gables laugh —

A few went out to help the Brook
That went to help the Sea —
Myself Conjectured were they Pearls —
What Necklace could be —

The Dust replaced, in Hoisted Roads —
The Birds jocoser sung —
The Sunshine threw his Hat away —
The Bushes — spangles flung —

The Breezes brought dejected Lutes —
And bathed them in the Glee —
Then Orient showed a single Flag,
And signed the Fete away —

∽

She staked her Feathers — Gained an Arc —
Debated — Rose again —
This time — beyond the estimate
Of Envy, or of Men —

And now, among Circumference —
Her steady Boat be seen —
At home — among the Billows — As
The Bough where she was born —

∽

Time feels so vast that were it not
For an Eternity —
I fear me this Circumference
Engross my Finity —

To His exclusion, who prepare
By Processes of Size
For the Stupendous Vision
Of his diameters —

ᑫᢙ

Expectation — is Contentment —
Gain — Satiety —
But Satiety — Conviction
Of Necessity

Of an Austere trait in Pleasure —
Good, without alarm
Is a too established Fortune —
Danger — deepens Sum —

ᑫᢙ

I felt a Cleaving in my Mind —
As if my Brain had split —
I tried to match it — Seam by Seam —
But could not make them fit.

The thought behind, I strove to join
Unto the thought before —
But Sequence ravelled out of Sound
Like Balls — upon a Floor.

∽

Fairer through Fading — as the Day
Into the Darkness dips away —
Half Her Complexion of the Sun —
Hindering — Haunting — Perishing —

Rallies Her Glow, like a dying Friend —
Teasing with glittering Amend —
Only to aggravate the Dark
Through an expiring — perfect — look —

∽

What I see not, I better see —
Through Faith — my Hazel Eye
Has periods of shutting —
But, No lid has Memory —

For frequent, all my sense obscured
I equally behold
As someone held a light unto
The Features so beloved —

And I arise — and in my Dream —
Do Thee distinguished Grace —
Till jealous Daylight interrupt —
And mar thy perfectness —

༄

The Loneliness One dare not sound —
And would as soon surmise
As in its Grave go plumbing
To ascertain the size —

The Loneliness whose worst alarm
Is lest itself should see —
And perish from before itself
For just a scrutiny —

The Horror not to be surveyed —
But skirted in the Dark —
With Consciousness suspended —
And Being under Lock —

I fear me this — is Loneliness —
The Maker of the soul
Its Caverns and its Corridors
Illuminate — or seal —

༄

To wait an Hour — is long —
If Love be just beyond —
To wait Eternity — is short —
If Love reward the end —

༄

Such is the Force of Happiness —
The Least — can lift a Ton
Assisted by its stimulus —

Who Misery — sustain —
No Sinew can afford —

The Cargo of Themselves —
Too infinite for Consciousness'
Slow capabilities.

⌒

Further in Summer than the Birds —
Pathetic from the Grass —
A Minor Nation celebrates
Its unobtrusive Mass —

No Ordinance be seen —
So gradual the Grace
A pensive Custom it becomes
Enlarging Loneliness —

'Tis Audiblest, at Dusk —
When Day's attempt is done —
And Nature nothing waits to do
But terminate in Tune —

Nor difference it knows
Of Cadence, or of Pause —
But simultaneous as Same —
The Service emphasize —

Nor know I when it cease —
At Candles, it is here —

When Sunrise is — that it is not —
Than this, I know no more —

The Earth has many keys —
Where Melody is not
Is the Unknown Peninsula —
Beauty — is Nature's Fact —

But Witness for Her Land —
And Witness for Her Sea —
The Cricket is Her utmost
Of Elegy, to Me —

⁓

The Soul's distinct connection
With immortality
Is best disclosed by Danger
Or quick Calamity —

As Lightning on a Landscape
Exhibits Sheets of Place —
Not yet suspected — but for Flash —
And Click — and Suddenness.

⁓

As Frost is best conceived
By force of its Result —
Affliction is inferred
By subsequent effect —

If when the sun reveal,
The Garden keep the Gash —
If as the Days resume
The wilted countenance

Cannot correct the crease
Or counteract the stain —
Presumption is Vitality
Was somewhere put in twain.

～

The Poets light but Lamps —
Themselves — go out —
The Wicks they stimulate —
If vital Light

Inhere as do the Suns —
Each Age a Lens
Disseminating their
Circumference —

Of Tolling Bell I ask the cause?
"A Soul has gone to Heaven"
I'm answered in a lonesome tone —
Is Heaven then a Prison?

That Bells should ring till all should know
A Soul had gone to Heaven
Would seem to me the more the way
A Good News should be given.

I made slow Riches but my Gain
Was steady as the Sun
And every Night, it numbered more
Than the preceding One

All Days, I did not earn the same
But my perceiveless Gain
Inferred the less by Growing than
The Sum that it had grown.

Unable are the Loved to die
For Love is Immortality,
Nay, it is Deity —

Unable they that love — to die
For Love reforms Vitality
Into Divinity.

&

A Light exists in Spring
Not present on the Year
At any other period —
When March is scarcely here

A Color stands abroad
On Solitary Fields
That Science cannot overtake
But Human Nature feels.

It waits upon the Lawn,
It shows the furthest Tree
Upon the furthest Slope you know
It almost speaks to you.

Then as Horizons step
Or Noons report away
Without the Formula of sound
It passes and we stay —

A quality of loss
Affecting our Content
As Trade had suddenly encroached
Upon a Sacrament.

c⌒ɔ

How far is it to Heaven?
As far as Death this way —
Of River or of Ridge beyond
Was no discovery.

How far is it to Hell?
As far as Death this way —
How far left hand the Sepulchre
Defies Topography.

c⌒ɔ

Two Travellers perishing in Snow
The Forests as they froze
Together heard them strengthening
Each other with the words

That Heaven if Heaven — must contain
What Either left behind
And then the cheer too solemn grew
For language, and the wind

Long steps across the features took
That Love had touched the Morn
With reverential Hyacinth —
The taleless Days went on

Till Mystery impatient drew
And those They left behind
Led absent, were procured of Heaven
As Those first furnished, said —

∽

Peace is a fiction of our Faith —
The Bells a Winter Night
Bearing the Neighbor out of Sound
That never did alight.

∽

The largest Fire ever known
Occurs each Afternoon —
Discovered is without surprise
Proceeds without concern —
Consumes and no report to men
An Occidental Town,
Rebuilt another morning
To be again burned down.

⌒

If I can stop one heart from breaking,
I shall not live in vain;
If I can ease one life the aching,
Or cool one pain,
Or help one fainting robin
Unto his nest again,
I shall not live in vain.

⌒

Air has no Residence, no Neighbor,
No Ear, no Door,
No Apprehension of Another
Oh, Happy Air!

Ethereal Guest at e'en an Outcast's Pillow —
Essential Host, in Life's faint, wailing Inn,
Later than Light thy Consciousness accost me
Till it depart, persuading Mine —

✺

Three Weeks passed since I had seen Her —
Some Disease had vext
'Twas with Text and Village Singing
I beheld Her next

And a Company — our pleasure
To discourse alone —
Gracious now to me as any —
Gracious unto none —

Borne without dissent of Either
To the Parish night —
Of the Separated Parties
Which be out of sight?

✺

I heard, as if I had no Ear
Until a Vital Word
Came all the way from Life to me
And then I knew I heard.

I saw, as if my Eye were on
Another, till a Thing
And now I know 'twas Light, because
It fitted them, came in.

I dwelt, as if Myself, were out,
My Body but within
Until a Might detected me
And set my kernel in.

And Spirit turned unto the Dust
"Old Friend, thou knowest me,"
And Time went out to tell the News
And met Eternity.

✺

Crumbling is not an instant's Act
A fundamental pause
Dilapidation's processes
Are organized Decays.

'Tis first a Cobweb on the Soul
A Cuticle of Dust
A Borer in the Axis
An Elemental Rust —

Ruin is formal — Devil's work
Consecutive and slow —
Fail in an instant, no man did
Slipping — is Crash's law.

∾

Up Life's Hill with my little Bundle
If I prove it steep —
If a Discouragement withhold me —
If my newest step

Older feel than the Hope that prompted —
Spotless be from blame
Heart that proposed as Heart that accepted
Homelessness, for Home —

∾

The Dying need but little, Dear,
A Glass of Water's all,
A Flower's unobtrusive Face
To punctuate the Wall,

A Fan, perhaps, a Friend's Regret
And Certainty that one
No color in the Rainbow
Perceive, when you are gone.

ᔕ

This Chasm, Sweet, upon my life
I mention it to you,
When Sunrise through a fissure drop
The Day must follow too.

If we demur, its gaping sides
Disclose as 'twere a Tomb
Ourself am lying straight wherein
The Favorite of Doom.

When it has just contained a Life
Then, Darling, it will close
And yet so bolder every Day
So turbulent it grows

I'm tempted half to stitch it up
With a remaining Breath
I should not miss in yielding, though
To Him, it would be Death —

And so I bear it big about
My Burial — before
A Life quite ready to depart
Can harass me no more —

ᙯ

The Sun and Moon must make their haste —
The Stars express around
For in the Zones of Paradise
The Lord alone is burned —

His Eye, it is the East and West —
The North and South when He
Do concentrate His Countenance
Like Glow Worms, flee away —

Oh Poor and Far —
Oh Hindred Eye
That hunted for the Day —
The Lord a Candle entertains
Entirely for Thee —

The Hollows round His eager Eyes
Were Pages where to read
Pathetic Histories — although
Himself had not complained.
Biography to All who passed
Of Unobtrusive Pain
Except for the italic Face
Endured, unhelped — unknown.

A narrow fellow in the grass
Occasionally rides;
You may have met him — did you not
His notice instant is,
The grass divides as with a comb,
A spotted shaft is seen,
And then it closes at your feet,
And opens further on.

He likes a boggy acre
A floor too cool for corn,
Yet when a boy and barefoot,
I more than once at noon

Have passed, I thought, a whip lash,
Unbraiding in the sun,
When stooping to secure it,
It wrinkled and was gone.

Several of nature's people
I know, and they know me;
I feel for them a transport
Of cordiality.
Yet never met this fellow,
Attended or alone,
Without a tighter breathing,
And zero at the bone.

‽

The bustle in a house
The morning after death
Is solemnest of industries
Enacted upon earth, —

The sweeping up the heart,
And putting love away
We shall not want to use again
Until eternity.

This is a Blossom of the Brain —
A small — italic Seed
Lodged by Design or Happening
The Spirit fructified —

Shy as the Wind of his Chambers
Swift as a Freshet's Tongue
So of the Flower of the Soul
Its process is unknown.

When it is found, a few rejoice
The Wise convey it Home
Carefully cherishing the spot
If other Flower become.

When it is lost, that Day shall be
The Funeral of God,
Upon his Breast, a closing Soul
The Flower of our Lord.

Gratitude — is not the mention
Of a Tenderness,

But its still appreciation
Out of Plumb of Speech.

When the Sea return no Answer
By the Line and Lead
Proves it there's no Sea, or rather
A remoter Bed?

        ∽

The Frost of Death was on the Pane —
"Secure your Flower" said he.
Like Sailors fighting with a Leak
We fought Mortality.

Our passive Flower we held to Sea —
To Mountain — To the Sun —
Yet even on his Scarlet shelf
To crawl the Frost begun —

We pried him back
Ourselves we wedged
Himself and her between,
Yet easy as the narrow Snake
He forked his way along

Till all her helpless beauty bent
And then our wrath begun —

We hunted him to his Ravine
We chased him to his Den —

We hated Death and hated Life
And nowhere was to go —
Than Sea and continent there is
A larger — it is Woe —

∽

The Merchant of the Picturesque
A Counter has and sales
But is within or negative
Precisely as the calls —
To Children he is small in price
And large in courtesy —
It suits him better than a check
Their artless currency —
Of Counterfeits he is so shy
Do one advance so near
As to behold his ample flight —

∽

These are the Nights that Beetles love —
From Eminence remote
Drives ponderous perpendicular
His figure intimate
The terror of the Children
The merriment of men
Depositing his Thunder
He hoists abroad again —
A Bomb upon the Ceiling
Is an improving thing —
It keeps the nerves progressive
Conjecture flourishing —
Too dear the Summer evening
Without discreet alarm —
Supplied by Entomology
With its remaining charm —

&

The Snow that never drifts —
The transient, fragrant snow
That comes a single time a Year
Is softly driving now —

So thorough in the Tree
At night beneath the star
That it was February's Foot
Experience would swear —

Like Winter as a Face
We stern and former knew
Repaired of all but Loneliness
By Nature's Alibi —

Were every storm so spice
The Value could not be —
We buy with contrast — Pang is good
As near as memory —

∽

The duties of the Wind are few,
To cast the ships, at Sea,
Establish March, the Floods escort,
And usher Liberty.

The pleasures of the Wind are broad,
To dwell Extent among,
Remain, or wander,
Speculate, or Forests entertain.

The kinsmen of the Wind are Peaks
Azof — the Equinox,
Also with Bird and Asteroid
A bowing intercourse.

The limitations of the Wind
Do he exist, or die,
Too wise he seems for Wakelessness,
However, know not I.

~

A not admitting of the wound
Until it grew so wide
That all my Life had entered it
And there were troughs beside —

A closing of the simple lid that opened to the sun
Until the tender Carpenter
Perpetual nail it down —

~

My Triumph lasted till the Drums
Had left the Dead alone
And then I dropped my Victory
And chastened stole along
To where the finished Faces
Conclusion turned on me
And then I hated Glory
And wished myself were They.

What is to be is best descried
When it has also been —
Could Prospect taste of Retrospect
The tyrannies of Men
Were Tenderer — diviner
The Transitive toward.
A Bayonet's contrition
Is nothing to the Dead.

⁓

Who goes to dine must take his Feast
Or find the Banquet mean —
The Table is not laid without
Till it is laid within.

For Pattern is the Mind bestowed
That imitating her
Our most ignoble Services
Exhibit worthier.

⁓

The Mountains stood in Haze —
The Valleys stopped below

And went or waited as they liked
The River and the Sky.

At leisure was the Sun —
His interests of Fire
A little from remark withdrawn —
The Twilight spoke the Spire,

So soft upon the Scene
The Act of evening fell
We felt how neighborly a Thing
Was the Invisible.

～

Step lightly on this narrow spot —
The broadest Land that grows
Is not so ample as the Breast
These Emerald Seams enclose.

Step lofty, for this name be told
As far as Cannon dwell
Or Flag subsist or Fame export
Her deathless Syllable.

～

Oh Shadow on the Grass,
Art thou a Step or not?
Go make thee fair my Candidate
My nominated Heart —
Oh Shadow on the Grass
While I delay to guess
Some other thou wilt consecrate —
Oh Unelected Face —

⁓

So much of Heaven has gone from Earth
That there must be a Heaven
If only to enclose the Saints
To Affidavit given.

The Missionary to the Mole
Must prove there is a Sky
Location doubtless he would plead
But what excuse have I?

Too much of Proof affronts Belief
The Turtle will not try
Unless you leave him — then return
And he has hauled away.

Risk is the Hair that holds the Tun
Seductive in the Air —
That Tun is hollow — but the Tun —
With Hundred Weights — to spare —

Too ponderous to suspect the snare
Espies that fickle chair
And seats itself to be let go
By that perfidious Hair —

The "foolish Tun" the Critics say —
While that delusive Hair
Persuasive as Perdition,
Decoys its Traveller.

⁓

Tell all the Truth but tell it slant —
Success in Circuit lies
Too bright for our infirm Delight
The Truth's superb surprise

As Lightning to the Children eased
With explanation kind

The Truth must dazzle gradually
Or every man be blind —

∽

A Word dropped careless on a Page
May stimulate an eye
When folded in perpetual seam
The Wrinkled Maker lie

Infection in the sentence breeds
We may inhale Despair
At distances of Centuries
From the Malaria —

∽

There is no Frigate like a Book
To take us Lands away
Nor any Coursers like a Page
Of prancing Poetry —
This Traverse may the poorest take
Without opress of Toll —
How frugal is the Chariot
That bears the Human soul

Longing is like the Seed
That wrestles in the Ground,
Believing if it intercede
It shall at length be found.

The Hour, and the Clime —
Each Circumstance unknown,
What Constancy must be achieved
Before it see the Sun!

Because that you are going
And never coming back
And I, however absolute,
May overlook your Track —

Because that Death is final,
However first it be,
This instant be suspended
Above Mortality —

Significance that each has lived
The other to detect

Discovery not God himself
Could now annihilate

Eternity, Presumption
The instant I perceive
That you, who were Existence
Yourself forgot to live —

The "Life that is" will then have been
A thing I never knew —
As Paradise fictitious
Until the Realm of you —

The "Life that is to be," to me,
A Residence too plain
Unless in my Redeemer's Face
I recognize your own —

Of Immortality who doubts
He may exchange with me
Curtailed by your obscuring Face
Of everything but He —

Of Heaven and Hell I also yield
The Right to reprehend
To whoso would commute this Face
For his less priceless Friend.

If "God is Love" as he admits
We think that me must be

Because he is a "jealous God"
He tells us certainly

If "All is possible with" him
As he besides concedes
He will refund us finally
Our confiscated Gods —

∽

While we were fearing it, it came —
But came with less of fear
Because that fearing it so long
Had almost made it fair —

There is a Fitting — a Dismay —
A Fitting — a Despair
'Tis harder knowing it is Due
Than knowing it is Here.

They Trying on the Utmost
The Morning it is new
Is Terribler than wearing it
A whole existence through.

∽

How many schemes may die
In one short Afternoon
Entirely unknown
To those they most concern —
The man that was not lost
Because by accident
He varied by a Ribbon's width
From his accustomed route —
The Love that would not try
Because beside the Door
It must be competitions
Some unsuspecting Horse was tied
Surveying his Despair

﹏

As Summer into Autumn slips
And yet we sooner say
"The Summer" than "the Autumn," lest
We turn the sun away,

And almost count it an Affront
The presence to concede
Of one however lovely, not
The one that we have loved —

So we evade the charge of Years
On one attempting shy

The Circumvention of the Shaft
Of Life's Declivity.

&

Not with a Club, the Heart is broken
Nor with a Stone —
A Whip so small you could not see it
I've known

To lash the Magic Creature
Till it fell,
Yet that Whip's Name
Too noble then to tell.

Magnanimous as Bird
By Boy descried —
Singing unto the Stone
Of which it died —

Shame need not crouch
In such an Earth as Ours —
Shame — stand erect —
The Universe is yours.

&

Let me not mar that perfect Dream
By an Auroral stain
But so adjust my daily Night
That it will come again.

Not when we know, the Power accosts —
The Garment of Surprise
Was all our timid Mother wore
At Home — in Paradise.

⤶

Upon a Lilac Sea
To toss incessantly
His Plush Alarm
Who fleeing from the Spring
The Spring avenging fling
To Dooms of Balm

⤶

Delight's Despair at setting
Is that Delight is less
Than the sufficing Longing
That so impoverish.

Enchantment's Perihelion
Mistaken oft has been
For the Authentic orbit
Of its Anterior Sun.

       ∽

Dreams are the subtle Dower
That make us rich an Hour —
Then fling us poor
Out of the purple Door
Into the Precinct raw
Possessed before —

       ∽

Long Years apart — can make no
Breach a second cannot fill —
The absence of the Witch does not
Invalidate the spell —

The embers of a Thousand Years
Uncovered by the Hand
That fondled them when they were Fire
Will stir and understand —

c⌒ɔ

The Bat is dun, with wrinkled Wings —
Like fallow Article —
And not a song pervade his Lips —
Or none perceptible.

His small Umbrella quaintly halved
Describing in the Air
An Arc alike inscrutable
Elate Philosopher.

Deputed from what Firmament —
Of what Astute Abode —
Empowered with what Malignity
Auspiciously withheld —

To his adroit Creator
Ascribe no less the praise —
Beneficent, believe me,
His Eccentricities —

c⌒ɔ

Trusty as the stars
Who quit their shining working

Prompt as when I lit them
In Genesis' new house,
Durable as dawn
Whose antiquated blossom
Makes a world's suspense
Perish and rejoice.

∽

How much the present moment means
To those who've nothing more —
The Fop — the Carp — the Atheist —
Stake an entire store
Upon a Moment's shallow Rim
While their commuted Feet
The Torrents of Eternity
Do all but inundate —

∽

Lay this Laurel on the One
Too intrinsic for Renown —
Laurel — veil your deathless tree —
Him you chasten, that is He!

What mystery pervades a well!
That water lives so far —
A neighbor from another world
Residing in a jar

Whose limit none have ever seen,
But just his lid of glass —
Like looking every time you please
In an abyss's face!

The grass does not appear afraid,
I often wonder he
Can stand so close and look so bold
At what is awe to me.

Related somehow they may be,
The sedge stands next the sea —
Where he is floorless
And does no timidity betray

But nature is a stranger yet;
The ones that cite her most
Have never passed her haunted house,
Nor simplified her ghost.

To pity those that know her not
Is helped by the regret

That those who know her, know her less
The nearer her they get.

∽

One Joy of so much anguish
Sweet nature has for me
I shun it as I do Despair
Or dear iniquity —
Why Birds, a Summer morning
Before the Quick of Day
Should stab my ravished spirit
With Dirks of Melody
Is part of an inquiry
That will receive reply
When Flesh and Spirit sunder
In Death's Immediately —

∽

It sounded as if the Streets were running
And then — the Streets stood still —
Eclipse — was all we could see at the Window
And Awe — was all we could feel.

By and by — the boldest stole out of his Covert
To see if Time was there —
Nature was in an Opal Apron,
Mixing fresher Air.

ॐ

Death is the supple Suitor
That wins at last —
It is a stealthy Wooing
Conducted first
By pallid innuendoes
And dim approach
But brave at last with Bugles
And a bisected Coach
It bears away in triumph
To Troth unknown
And Kindred as responsive
As Porcelain.

ॐ

Hope is a subtle Glutton —
He feeds upon the Fair —

And yet — inspected closely
What Abstinence is there —

His is the Halcyon Table —
That never seats but One —
And whatsoever is consumed
The same amount remain —

∽

If wrecked upon the Shoal of Thought
How is it with the Sea?
The only Vessel that is shunned
Is safe — Simplicity —

∽

The fascinating chill that music leaves
Is Earth's corroboration
Of Ecstasy's impediment —
'Tis Rapture's germination
In timid and tumultuous soil
A fine — estranging creature —
To something upper wooing us
But not to our Creator —

Glass was the Street — in tinsel Peril
Tree and Traveller stood —
Filled was the Air with merry venture
Hearty with Boys the Road —

Shot the lithe Sleds like shod vibrations
Emphasized and gone
It is the Past's supreme italic
Makes this Present mean —

∽

The Face in evanescence lain
Is more distinct than ours —
And ours surrendered for its sake
As Capsules are for Flower's —
Or is it the confiding sheen
Dissenting to enamor us
Of Detriment divine?

∽

You cannot make Remembrance grow
When it has lost its Root —
The tightening the Soil around
And setting it upright
Deceives perhaps the Universe
But not retrieves the Plant —
Real Memory, like Cedar Feet
Is shod with Adamant —
Nor can you cut Remembrance down
When it shall once have grown —
Its Iron Buds will sprout anew
However overthrown —

My country need not change her gown,
Her triple suit as sweet
As when 'twas cut at Lexington,
And first pronounced "a fit."

Great Britain disapproves, "the stars";
Disparagement discreet, —
There's something in their attitude
That taunts her bayonet.

A faded Boy — in sallow Clothes
Who drove a lonesome Cow
To pastures of Oblivion —
A statesman's Embryo —

The Boys that whistled are extinct —
The Cows that fed and thanked
Remanded to a Ballad's Barn
Or Clover's Retrospect —

∽

The Bird her punctual music brings
And lays it in its place —
Its place is in the Human Heart
And in the Heavenly Grace —
What respite from her thrilling toil
Did Beauty ever take —
But Work might be electric Rest
To those that Magic make —

∽

The Butterfly upon the Sky,
That doesn't know its Name

And hasn't any tax to pay
And hasn't any Home
Is just as high as you and I,
And higher, I believe,
So soar away and never sigh
And that's the way to grieve —

৩

Sweet Pirate of the heart,
Not Pirate of the Sea,
What wrecketh thee?
Some spice's Mutiny —
Some Attar's perfidy?
Confide in me.

৩

No matter where the Saints abide,
They make their Circuit fair
Behold how great a Firmament
Accompanies a Star.

Those — dying then,
Knew where they went —
They went to God's Right Hand —
That Hand is amputated now
And God cannot be found —

The abdication of Belief
Makes the Behavior small —
Better an ignis fatuus
Than no illume at all —

He ate and drank the precious Words —
His Spirit grew robust —
He knew no more that he was poor,
Nor that his frame was Dust —

He danced along the dingy Days
And this Bequest of Wings
Was but a Book — What Liberty
A loosened spirit brings —

No ladder needs the bird but skies
To situate its wings,
Nor any leader's grim baton
Arraigns it as it sings.
The implements of bliss are few —
As Jesus says of Him,
"Come unto me" the moiety
That wafts the cherubim.

The Lassitudes of Contemplation
Beget a force
They are the spirit's still vacation
That him refresh —
The Dreams consolidate in action —
What mettle fair

There came a Wind like a Bugle —
It quivered through the Grass
And a Green Chill upon the Heat
So ominous did pass
We barred the Windows and the Doors
As from an Emerald Ghost —
The Doom's electric Moccasin
That very instant passed —
On a strange Mob of panting Trees
And Fences fled away
And Rivers where the Houses ran
Those looked that lived — that Day —
The Bell within the steeple wild
The flying tidings told —
How much can come
And much can go,
And yet abide the World!

&

The Spirit lasts — but in what mode —
Below, the Body speaks,
But as the Spirit furnishes —
Apart, it never talks —
The Music in the Violin
Does not emerge alone
But Arm in Arm with Touch, yet Touch
Alone — is not a Tune —

The Spirit lurks within the Flesh
Like Tides within the Sea
That make the Water live, estranged
What would the Either be?
Does that know — now — or does it cease —
That which to this is done,
Resuming at a mutual date
With every future one?
Instinct pursues the Adamant,
Exacting this Reply —
Adversity if it may be, or
Wild Prosperity,
The Rumor's Gate was shut so tight
Before my Mind was sown,
Not even a Prognostic's Push
Could make a Dent thereon —

⌁

A Drunkard cannot meet a Cork
Without a Revery —
And so encountering a Fly
This January Day
Jamaicas of Remembrance stir
That send me reeling in —
The moderate drinker of Delight
Does not deserve the spring —
Of juleps, part are in the Jug

And more are in the joy —
Your connoisseur in Liquours
Consults the Bumble Bee —

⌒

Who is it seeks my Pillow Nights —
With plain inspecting face —
"Did you" or "Did you not," to ask —
'Tis "Conscience" — Childhood's Nurse —

With Martial Hand she strokes the Hair
Upon my wincing Head —
"All" Rogues "shall have their part in" what —
The Phosphorous of God —

⌒

Not knowing when the Dawn will come,
I open every Door,
Or has it Feathers, like a Bird,
Or Billows, like a Shore —

Talk not to me of Summer Trees
The foliage of the mind
A Tabernacle is for Birds
Of no corporeal kind
And winds do go that way at noon
To their Ethereal Homes
Whose Bugles call the least of us
To undepicted Realms

Beauty crowds me till I die
Beauty mercy have on me
But if I expire today
Let it be in sight of thee —

There is a solitude of space
A solitude of sea
A solitude of death, but these

Society shall be
Compared with that profounder site
That polar privacy
A soul admitted to itself —
Finite infinity.

∽

Fame is a fickle food
Upon a shifting plate
Whose table once a
Guest but not
The second time is set.

Whose crumbs the crows inspect
And with ironic caw
Flap past it to the
Farmer's Corn —
Men eat of it and die.

∽

I did not reach Thee
But my feet slip nearer every day
Three Rivers and a Hill to cross

One Desert and a Sea
I shall not count the journey one
When I am telling thee.

Two deserts, but the Year is cold
So that will help the sand
One desert crossed —
The second one
Will feel as cool as land
Sahara is too little price
To pay for thy Right hand.

The Sea comes last — Step merry, feet,
So short we have to go —
To play together we are prone,
But we must labor now,
The last shall be the lightest load
That we have had to draw.

The Sun goes crooked —
That is Night
Before he makes the bend.
We must have passed the Middle Sea —
Almost we wish the End
Were further off —
Too great it seems
So near the Whole to stand.

We step like Plush,
We stand like snow,
The waters murmur new.

Three rivers and the Hill are passed —
Two deserts and the sea!
Now Death usurps my Premium
And gets the look at Thee.

*

Sometimes with the Heart
Seldom with the Soul
Scarcer once with the Might
Few — love at all.

*

They talk as slow as Legends grow
No mushroom is their mind
But foliage of sterility
Too stolid for the wind —

They laugh as wise as Plots of Wit
Predestined to unfold
The point with bland prevision
Portentously untold.

A Cap of Lead across the sky
Was tight and surly drawn
We could not find the mighty Face
The Figure was withdrawn —

A Chill came up as from a shaft
Our noon became a well
A Thunder storm combines the charms
Of Winter and of Hell.

'Twas comfort in her Dying Room
To hear the living Clock —
A short relief to have the wind
Walk boldly up and knock —
Diversion from the Dying Theme
To hear the children play —
But wrong the more
That these could live
And this of ours must die.

As subtle as tomorrow
That never came,
A warrant, a conviction,
Yet but a name.

∽

Did life's penurious length
Italicize its sweetness,
The men that daily live
Would stand so deep in joy
That it would clog the cogs
Of that revolving reason
Whose esoteric belt
Protects our sanity.

∽

Her face was in a bed of hair,
Like flowers in a plot —
Her hand was whiter than the sperm
That feeds the sacred light.
Her tongue more tender than the tune
That totters in the leaves —

Who hears may be incredulous,
Who witnesses, believes.

❦

Love can do all but raise the Dead
I doubt if even that
From such a giant were withheld
Were flesh equivalent

But love is tired and must sleep,
And hungry and must graze
And so abets the shining Fleet
Till it is out of gaze.

❦

The waters chased him as he fled,
Not daring look behind —
A billow whispered in his Ear,
"Come home with me, my friend —
My parlor is of shriven glass,
My pantry has a fish
For every palate in the Year" —

To this revolting bliss
The object floating at his side
Made no distinct reply.

❧

Softened by Time's consummate plush,
How sleek the woe appears
That threatened childhood's citadel
And undermined the years.

Bisected now, by bleaker griefs,
We envy the despair
That devastated childhood's realm,
So easy to repair.

❧

To make a prairie it takes a clover and one bee,
One clover, and a bee,
And revery.
The revery alone will do,
If bees are few.

Sweet hours have perished here,
This is a timid room —
Within its precincts hopes have played
Now fallow in the tomb.

Fame is a bee.
  It has a song —
It has a sting —
  Ah, too, it has a wing.

The saddest noise, the sweetest noise,
The maddest noise that grows, —
The birds, they make it in the spring,
At night's delicious close.

Between the March and April line —
That magical frontier

Beyond which summer hesitates,
Almost too heavenly near.

It makes us think of all the dead
That sauntered with us here,
By separation's sorcery
Made cruelly more dear.

It makes us think of what we had,
And what we now deplore.
We almost wish those siren throats
Would go and sing no more.

An ear can break a human heart
As quickly as a spear,
We wish the ear had not a heart
So dangerously near.

Index of First Lines